Contents

069394

KT-198-926

Foreword

Acknowledgements
The publishers would like to thank Speedo (Europe) Ltd for their photographic contribution to this book.

Photographs on the front cover, back cover, inside front cover, inside back cover and pages 5, 15, 16, 17, 21, 33, 47 courtesy of Allsport UK Ltd. Photograph on page 25 courtesy of Sporting Pictures (UK) Ltd.

Everyone should learn how to swim, whatever their age. Children should be introduced to water as early as possible so that they become happy and confident in the water before reaching school age.

Swimming is a sport in which people of all ages and levels of ability can participate, and from which they can derive a great deal of beneficial exercise and enjoyment.

It is also essential to be able to swim competently if you wish to participate in other exciting water-based activities.

This book sets out clearly the skills and knowledge required at each stage of learning how to swim, from developing initial water confidence to performing the main strokes and learning how to dive. Parents will find that it includes useful advice on helping even very young children to feel at home in the water, so that they come to the swimming pool ready to enjoy developing their swimming skills.

In schools, swimming is an important part of the National Curriculum for Physical Education, particularly up to the age of 11 years. By the time children leave primary school – at the end of Key Stage 2 – they should be able to swim at least 25 m and demonstrate an understanding of water safety. This book should provide an excellent resource for both parent and teacher in helping children to achieve these objectives.

The Amateur Swimming Association has produced a guide which is clearly and simply written, and illustrated with informative colour photographs and diagrams. It deals not only with the very basics for child and novice, but also offers sound advice to more experienced swimmers who wish to improve their swimming skills and understanding of water safety.

Beginning to swim

Early training

From the earliest days, bath-time provides babies with the experience of immersion. With the gentle support of parents they can enjoy splashing, kicking and floating.

It is important to remember that there should be no irritants in the water, and that the water temperature should be comfortable so that any activities can be carried out in a relaxed atmosphere with the emphasis on enjoyment.

As babies grow and are able to use the family bath, they will make movements on their front and on their back with support. They can be encouraged to blow bubbles in the water, to move around while playing with familiar toys, and to retrieve submerged objects. Gradually they will discover the buoyancy that water offers. This is an important first step in beginning to swim.

Since a happy child–parent relationship is an important factor when young children are learning how to swim, parents should encourage a liking for water by making sure that bath-time is a pleasant, shared activity. At no time should young children be left unattended in the bath.

Early swimming-pool experience

It is generally recommended that babies be taken to the swimming pool only after they have completed two out of three triple and polio vaccinations, which stimulate the immune system to resist disease. By this time the baby will be six months old.

A parent-and-baby swimming class is an ideal way to make the transition from home to the swimming pool. All non-swimmers, whether child or adult, will benefit from a preliminary 'dry' visit to the swimming pool to observe others learning how to swim. This visit should familiarise the non-swimmer with the swimming-pool environment and help them to appreciate that learning to swim can be fun.

There are two main types of swimming pool: the traditional rectangular pool and the modern, free-form leisure pool. Leisure pools are usually equipped with many exciting features such as slides, flumes and wave-making machines, and are fun and exciting places to visit. Whatever the type of pool, warm, shallow water and relatively quiet conditions are the most conducive to learning how to swim.

For younger children, the size, unfamiliar noise and the presence of others may make the swimming pool rather overwhelming at first. Parents should not be in too much of a hurry; they should wait until children show a willingness to enter the water, allowing them time to become familiar with the new environment. A happy first experience is the key to future success and enjoyment.

To ensure a happy and successful first experience, the parent should provide the child with plenty of support.

This can be achieved with the assistance of well-fitting buoyancy aids if the child is too small to reach the bottom of the pool, and with gentle support provided by the parents.

This support will give the child confidence to make exploratory movements in the water. Some children will adopt a horizontal position, while others will be more upright. From these positions the child can be encouraged to make simple kicking movements of the legs and pulling movements of the arms, thus experiencing a feeling of propulsion.

Progress can be made by showing children how the parents can use their limbs to kick and pull: they can then imitate these actions. If necessary, parents can help their children to learn the correct movements by holding their arms or legs and guiding them through the water. Repetition of movements should follow, accompanied by constant praise and encouragement. At this stage it is easier if all limb movements are made under the water. During these activities children should breathe naturally and gradually be encouraged to breathe out into the water.

Confidence and learning ability should be assessed continually, and the next step set at just beyond the child's current capabilities. Initially, time spent in the water should be brief, especially if the child is showing signs of feeling cold or tired. It is better that the child leaves the pool wanting to stay in longer, rather than feeling distressed.

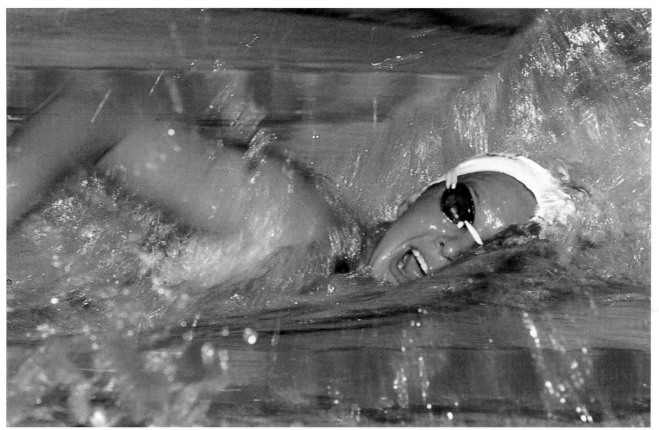

Developing independence

As progress is made, the need for buoyancy aids will diminish. Gradually reduce the amount of air in the aids, eventually removing them completely so that the child moves through the water completely unaided. The child is now *beginning to swim*.

Before children can be allowed to move freely around the shallow end of the pool, they must be able to regain a standing position from both the front and back swimming positions. This is an important safety measure.

Regaining the standing position

On the front

Press downwards with outstretched arms and hands (with palms facing down). Tilt the head back and bend the knees forwards. As the body becomes upright, push the feet downwards to stand, while using the arms to help maintain balance (*see* fig. 1).

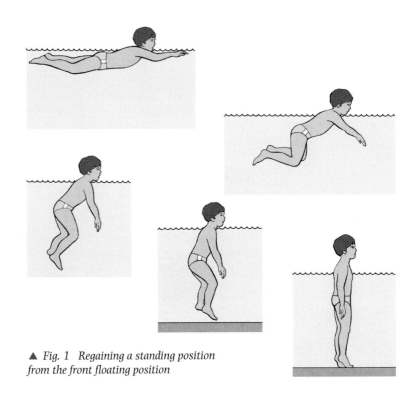

▲ *Fig. 1 Regaining a standing position from the front floating position*

On the back

Start by lifting the head forwards, pressing down with the arms and, at the same time, raising the knees towards the chest. As the body rotates to an upright position, turn palms to face the feet and scoop the arms forwards and upwards to assist the movement before pushing the feet downwards to stand (*see* fig. 2).

Once beginners have mastered the skill of standing from both the front and the back floating positions, they are ready to progress to *pushing and gliding*.

This enables the beginner to experience movement through the water in a stretched and streamlined position, which is fundamental to all swimming strokes.

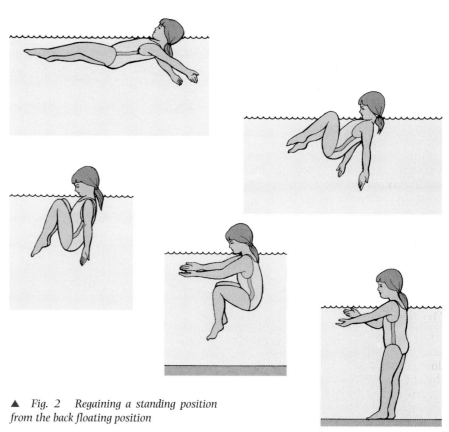

▲ *Fig. 2   Regaining a standing position from the back floating position*

The front glide

Starting from a standing position, with one foot slightly in front of the other, arms extended forwards and shoulders submerged, lean forwards and push along the surface and glide. Keep your head in line with your body, so that the top of your head is always at water-level (*see* fig. 3).

To increase the distance, start with your back against the pool side. Plant one foot firmly on the wall of the pool to obtain a stronger push (*see* fig. 4).

▲ *Fig. 3   Front glide from standing*

▼ *Fig. 4   Push and glide on front*

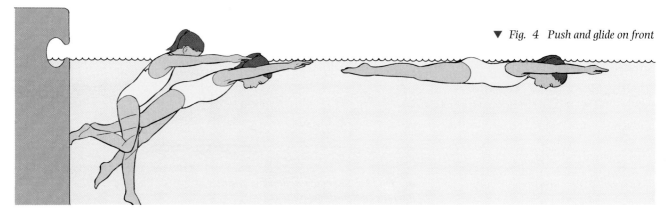

The back glide

From a standing position, with one foot slightly to the rear of the other, lower your body until your shoulders are submerged. Keep your arms outspread to assist balance. Then lean gently backwards and at the same time push into a glide. The back of your head should rest in the water. Bring your arms to your sides (*see* fig. 5).

To obtain greater distance, start with your hands grasping the scum-trough, rail or pool side and your feet placed firmly against the wall of the pool (knees just below the surface). By releasing your hands from the pool side and pushing steadily with your legs, a gliding position – in which your body should remain flat – can be attained (*see* fig. 6). Later, in order to gain more streamlining and greater distance, the push can be made with your arms extended beyond your head (hands together).

Gliding and standing practices can be combined, so that when attempts are made to swim on the front or back a return to the standing position can be made with complete confidence.

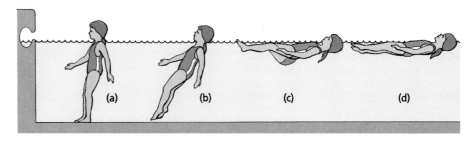

▲ *Fig. 5 Back glide from standing*

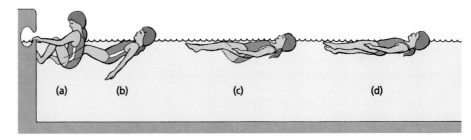

▲ *Fig. 6 Push and glide on back*

The paddle strokes

As confidence develops, the time will arrive for attempting basic actions for propulsion on the front and the back. These usually take the form of the front paddle (formerly called the dog paddle) and the back paddle.

Front paddle

The learner lies in the front floating position. The leg action is similar to the alternating up and down movement used for the front crawl. The arm action, however, takes place totally underwater; alternate arms are pulled downwards and backwards from the forward position, and then recovered by stretching the hands forwards from close to the chest to a point in advance of the shoulders. Initially, the swimmer will probably make short arm movements, but as confidence grows these actions will become longer and more powerful. The front paddle action is shown in fig. 7.

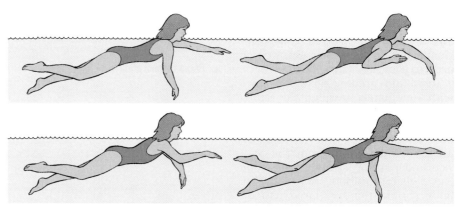

▲ *Fig. 7   Front paddle*

Back paddle and sculling

The learner lies in the back floating position. The leg action is similar to the alternating up and down movement used for the back crawl. In the early stages, arm movements usually consist of simultaneous sweeping actions towards the feet. Whilst this action produces considerable power, the recovery also creates a great deal of resistance. Gradually, the learner should try to keep the arms closer to the thighs so that the movements become familiar, figure-of-eight sculling actions. As the hands move away from the body, the leading edges (little fingers) are raised so that the palms are facing outwards and downwards. The leading edges on the inward movements (thumbs) are again raised, so that the palms face inwards and downwards. At the outer and innermost points in the action the wrists rotate to change the pitch of the palms. The arms remain fairly straight and without undue tension (*see* fig. 8).

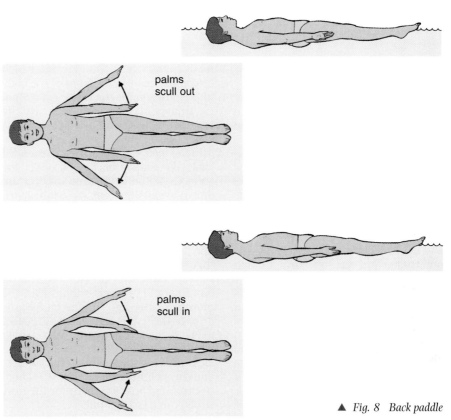

palms
scull out

palms
scull in

▲ *Fig. 8 Back paddle*

11

The breast stroke

Breast stroke sequence

This is the oldest of the four major strokes and is frequently used in recreational swimming, lifesaving and competition.

Before starting the stroke, the swimmer is on their front in a streamlined and horizontal position, shoulders parallel to the surface of the water. The head is in line with the body, and looking ahead along, or just below the surface of the water. The arms are extended in front and close together underwater; the legs are trailed out behind, straight and together (*see* fig. 9a).

The stroke begins with the arms pulling outwards, backwards and downwards to a point just in front of the shoulders. The legs remain stretched out behind (*see* figs 9b and 9c). In front of the shoulder-line the hands begin to sweep inwards with a swirling action, coming close together with the elbows close to the body

ready to start the recovery action which brings the arms to the front of the body in preparation for the next arm action. At this point the swimmer usually breathes in, as the mouth is clear of the water (*see* fig. 9d).

In the recovery, the arms are extended forwards, usually on or just under the surface. At the same time the feet are drawn towards the seat, hip-width apart, toes pointing backwards and knees well behind the hip-line (*see* fig. 9e).

As the arm recovery nears completion the feet turn outwards and the legs thrust vigorously backwards and slightly outwards in an accelerating movement. The heels should lead the movement (*see* fig. 9f). The backwards drive of the legs is completed as the feet follow a curved pathway with a final whip-like action. The feet finish the kick, with the toes pointing backwards, and the swimmer glides in a stretched, streamlined position ready for the next stroke cycle (*see* fig. 9a).

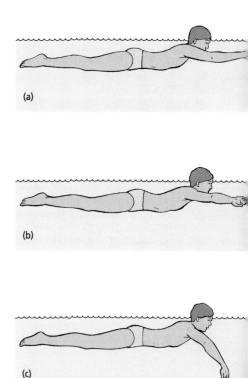

(a)

(b)

(c)

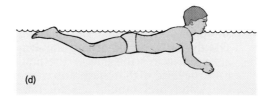

(d)

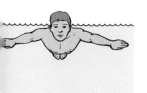

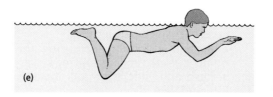

(e)

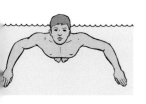

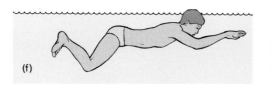

(f)

Practices

Body position

- Holding the rail or trough, practise the leg action briefly.
- With a float held out in front, swim across the width of the pool using legs only.
- Push and glide, followed by leg action only.

Arm action

- Standing in shallow water with shoulders submerged, practise the arm action.
- Walk slowly through the water, shoulders submerged and leaning slightly forwards, practising the arm action.

Breathing

- Walk slowly through the water, shoulders submerged and leaning slightly forwards, practising the arm action. Towards the end of the pull, raise the head so that the mouth clears the water and inhalation can take place.

Timing

- Push and glide, adding one arm cycle followed by the leg kick.
- Repeat, gradually increasing the number of arm actions and leg kicks.
- Push and glide, arm pull, breathe, kick and then glide.
- Breathe every stroke cycle.
- Increase the distance swum to establish a comfortable rhythm.

Points for attention

Body position

- Aim for a stretched, streamlined and near-horizontal position. Keep the head steady and the shoulders square; hips just below the surface; legs extended; toes pointed.

Leg action

- Heels towards the seat; feet turned out; heels lead the backward drive.
- The leg recovery takes place underwater. The feet must be turned outwards for the final drive; the leg kick must be simultaneous and symmetrical.
- Keep the legs behind the line of the hips at all times.

Arm action

- Keep the hands in view all the time. Press strongly sideways, downwards and backwards, recovering smoothly; pull in front of the shoulders.

Breathing

- Inhale as the arms complete their pull; exhale as they recover. Keep the head steady and the shoulders square.

Timing

- Keep the pull in front of the shoulders.
- Work to the rhythm of pull/breathe/kick/glide, with the emphasis on a strong kick backwards and a smooth glide to follow.
- As the arms are extended forwards, the legs drive backwards vigorously.

In competition, from the beginning of the first arm stroke after the start and after each turn, the body must be kept horizontal and the shoulders parallel with the water surface. All hand and feet movements must be simultaneous and in the same horizontal plane without any alternating movements. Part of the head must be above the water-level during each complete stroke cycle (except when starting and turning). Up-and-down movements of the legs are not allowed.

The front crawl

The front crawl is the fastest of all the swimming strokes. Propulsion takes place continuously.

Front crawl sequence

Throughout the stroke the swimmer should maintain a horizontal and streamlined body position, with the head in line with the body, eyes looking forwards and downwards and legs and feet extended. The leg kick is alternating and vertical, with legs passing close together. The movement starts in the hips and finishes with a whip-like action of the feet. The arm action is alternating and continuous. Propulsion is produced as the hand gradually accelerates downwards, inwards and finally upwards through the water. The arm recovers over the water with a high elbow movement, extending forwards slightly in preparation for re-entry.

Refer to figure 10 on pages 18–19. The right hand enters the water in front of the head and mid-way between the shoulder and the head (*see* fig. 10a). As the right arm sweeps downwards, the left sweeps upwards through the water into the recovery (*see* figs 10b and 10c). The strong downsweep of the right arm is balanced as the left leg kicks down (see fig. 10c). After the downsweep, the right arm sweeps inwards whilst the left completes the recovery (*see* fig. 10d).

As the left hand extends forwards to start the downsweep, the right arm sweeps upwards towards the recovery. During this phase the head is turned to the right, synchronised with the natural roll of the body (*see* fig. 10e). This enables the swimmer to inhale as the right arm recovers (*see* fig. 10f). (While moving through the water at speed, the head creates a bow wave and a trough behind it which enables the swimmer to inhale clear of the water without lifting the head.) After breathing in, the eyes look forwards again (*see* fig. 10g). The sequence is then repeated. Some swimmers find it natural to breathe with the head turned to the left. This is quite normal.

Practices

Body position

- Push and glide, as previously described.

Leg action

- Practise the leg action briefly at the pool side, holding the rail or trough.
- Push and glide, with or without a float, across the width of the pool and add the leg action.

Arm action

- Leaning forwards in shallow water with shoulders submerged, copy a demonstration of the arm action.
- Push and glide, add the leg action, and then introduce one complete arm cycle.
- Repeat, increasing the number of full stroke-cycles. Hold the breath to maintain good body poise.

Breathing

- Practise standing in shallow water, leaning forwards and grasping the rail or trough with one hand, with the face in the water. Breathe out into the water, then turn the head away from the supporting arm to breathe in quickly. Return the head to the forward position and repeat the practice.
- Hold a float. Push off and add a leg kick. Use one arm to pull. Turn the head to breathe as the arm sweeps upwards. Change hands.
- Swim a full stroke, attempting one or two breaths during each width.

Timing

- Normally there are six leg kicks to each complete arm-cycle, but variations of this are acceptable as long as the leg action balances that of the arm action (for example, four kicks to each arm-cycle).

▼ *Fig. 10 Front crawl sequence – viewed from the side and from the front*

(a)

(b)

(c)

(d)

(e)

(f)

(g)

Points for attention

Body position

- Aim for a stretched, streamlined and horizontal position.

Leg action

- Swing from the hips; make the legs 'long'.
- Legs straight and close together; ankles loose; feel the kick passing through the knee and ending in a whip-like action of the foot.

Arm action

- Entry in advance of the head, between the centre-line and the shoulder; thumb and fingers first, elbow high.
- After entry the sequence is: downwards/inwards/upwards.
- Aim for a smooth, flowing action, with relaxed arm recovery over the water.

Breathing

- Water should be level with the forehead. Eyes open, looking forwards.
- Breathe out through the nose and mouth into the water.
- Turn the head so that the mouth is just clear of the water when inhaling.
- Turn the head to whichever side is preferred. Breathe as the arm on the same side is completing the upsweep action immediately before the recovery, and as the other arm is about to start the downsweep.

Timing

- Frequent practices of part- and full-stroke of short duration are preferable to extended but infrequent practices. As an efficient style develops, so should the ability to increase the distances swum.

In competition, front crawl is invariably the stroke which is performed in freestyle events. When turning or finishing, a swimmer may touch the wall with any part of the body.

The back crawl

This stroke resembles the front crawl in that the arm and leg movements are of the alternating type, allowing continuous propulsion. The arms recover over the water, in what is sometimes called a 'windmill' action, as the legs kick upwards and downwards. Throughout the stroke-cycle the body maintains a near-horizontal position, with the back of the head pillowed in the water and the hips just below the surface.

Although this stroke is not as fast as the front crawl, when performed well it can be graceful and fluent.

Back crawl sequence

Refer to figure 11 on pages 22–23. The swimmer maintains a flat and stream-lined body position, with the head in line with the body as the left arm enters the water ready to sweep downwards and outwards. At this point, the right arm has finished the second downward sweep and is about to leave the water for recovery (*see* fig. 11a).

As the left arm sweeps downwards and outwards it bends gradually at the elbow. The right arm is lifted upwards through a circular pathway (*see* fig. 11b). The left arm continues to bend as it sweeps upwards, reaching an angle of approximately 90°. The right arm is now overhead (*see* fig. 11c).

The left arm now sweeps downwards once again to complete its propulsive phase, as the right arm is extended, entering the water directly in advance of the shoulder (*see* fig. 11d) to begin its propulsive phase (*see* fig. 11e). (The position is similar to that shown in fig. 11b, but with the arms – and legs – in the opposite positions.)

Practices

Body position

• Push off and glide on the back, arms held at the side of the body.
• Repeat with the arms extended beyond the head.

Leg action

• With a float under each arm, push off and add the leg action.
• With a float held at arm's length over your lower thighs, glide into position and add the leg action.
• Repeat the leg action – arms at the side, with or without sculling.

Arm action

• Push and glide from the pool side, add the leg action to establish body poise, and then introduce the arms.
• Attempt a few strokes at a time. Increase the distance swum gradually.

Breathing

• While swimming full-stroke, breathe regularly; breathe in as one arm recovers and breathe out as the other recovers.

Timing

• There are usually six leg beats to one complete cycle of the arms.

▼ *Fig. 11 Back crawl sequence – viewed from the side and from the front*

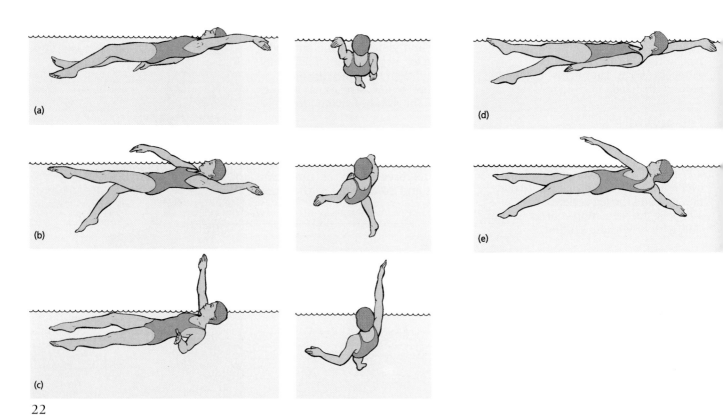

(a)

(b)

(c)

(d)

(e)

Points for attention

Body position

- Keep the back of the head in the water. Attempt to keep the hips at the surface.
- Keep the body flat, with arms and legs extended.

Leg action

- Move the legs from the hips.
- Keep the knees below the water surface. The legs should feel 'stretched and long' with the ankles flexed and loose.
- The toes should just break the surface.

Arm action

- Maintain a continuous, alternating arm action with one arm in an approximately opposite position to the other.
- Keep the actions flowing with a relaxed arm recovery.

Breathing

- Establish a regular breathing rhythm, then maintain it.

Timing

- Aim for continuity of action without any pauses.

In competition, swimmers must remain on their back until approaching the end of the course. They may turn on to their front to turn but must then surface on their back.

The butterfly stroke

The butterfly is the second-fastest stroke and the most recently developed. It is usually the last to be learned because it requires a high degree of strength, mobility and coordination. The swimmer is in a prone position, moving the arms and legs simultaneously and continuously. The arms recover over the water as the legs kick together, upwards and downwards in the vertical plane. The body moves in an undulating or dolphin-like pattern with the head rising above the water to breathe at the end of the underwater arm-pull. The hands trace a series of sculling actions in the water, sweeping outwards, downwards, inwards and finally outwards again to exit the water by the thighs.

Butterfly stroke sequence

Refer to figure 12 on pages 26–27. The hands enter the water with the thumbs and fingers first, about shoulder-width apart. The legs are beginning the first down beat (*see* fig. 12a).

At the end of the outsweep, the arms start the downsweep with elbows uppermost as the legs complete the first down beat (*see* fig. 12b).

The arms have completed the down and insweep and the legs have risen to the surface in readiness for the next propulsive down kick (*see* fig. 12c).

After the arms have passed the line of the shoulders, they sweep outwards and accelerate to their fastest underwater speed. The legs are beginning the second down beat (*see* fig. 12d).

As an extension of the final outsweep of the hands and arms, the elbows lead the recovery. The legs finish their second downward thrust. The upper body is at its highest position, making it easier for the swimmer to inhale at this stage (*see* fig. 12e).

The arms recover low with the elbows slightly bent in preparation for the entry. The legs return to the surface while the head moves back into the water (*see* fig. 12f).

Practices

Body position

● Push off and glide on the front, on the back and on the side, undulating like a fish to increase the distance covered gradually.

Leg action

● Holding the pool rail, briefly practise a front-crawl-type leg action with the feet and ankles together. (Repeat this action holding a float with arms extended in front.)
● Repeat this action without support, keeping the arms alongside the body.
● Repeat, but using a short breast stroke arm action.

Arm action

● Standing firmly with the body bent forwards and the shoulders in the water, practise the arm action.

Breathing

● Practise the arm action with the face in the water. Then raise the mouth forwards to breathe in as the arms push the body out of the water.

Timing

● Push off and glide. Perform two leg kicks followed by two more with a propulsive action, and recovery of the arms.
● Repeat, increasing the number of cycles. Gradually introduce breathing into every cycle.

▼ *Fig. 12   Butterfly sequence – viewed from the side and from the front*

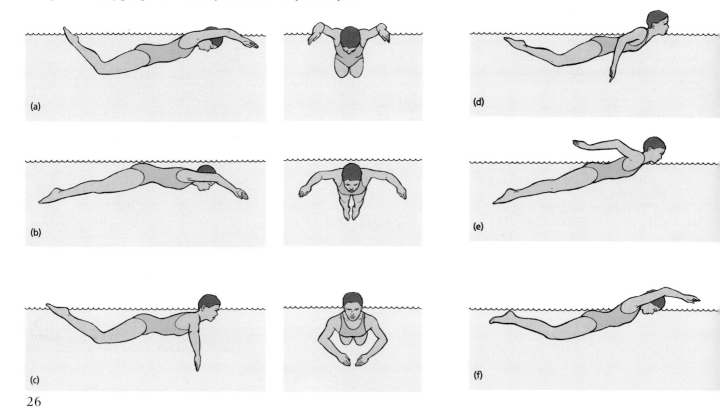

Points for attention

Body position

● Use this stroke over short distances only. Initiate the movement from the hips. Keep the body flat.

Leg action

● Remember that the leg action helps to maintain the required flat body position. Kick from the hips, drive the feet down vigorously and maintain a continuous action.
● Try to maintain relaxed ankles whilst kicking.
● After a number of kicks, use a short breast stroke arm action to allow a breath to be taken, then repeat the kicking action.

Arm action

● Try to ensure the arms enter the water with thumbs and fingers first. Feel the arms sweeping back through the water to recover with elbows uppermost in a 'flinging' action so that the hands enter the water about shoulder-width apart.

Breathing

● Hold the breath and then exhale 'explosively' immediately before breathing in. Do this at the end of the upsweep when the mouth is clear of the water.

Timing

● Hold the breath, keep the head down and try to maintain a flat body position.
● Make the first kick as the arms begin the outsweep, and the second as the arms are completing the upsweep.

In competition, all movements of the arms must be simultaneous. The arms must be taken forwards over the water and brought back on or under the surface. The body must be kept on the breast, with shoulders horizontal from the beginning of the first arm action after the start and after a turn. All movements of the feet must be simultaneous. Upward and downward movement of the legs and feet are permitted but there must be no alternating movement.

Diving

Diving is a popular activity. A number of serious accidents, however, have highlighted the associated dangers.

Accidents at swimming pools are rare but the most common ones are caused by diving into shallow water or by collision with other swimmers. In open water, accidents usually occur when people dive into water of unknown depth (usually because of murky conditions). Collisions with submerged obstacles or with the bottom then result.

Because of the dangers associated with diving, this section will only discuss practices for learning how to dive (up to and including the plunge dive).

Diving should only be conducted in the presence of a knowledgeable and experienced teacher in a swimming pool of suitable water depth.

Safety reminders

Before diving, take great care to ensure that the water is deep enough and that the diving area is clear of swimmers. 'No Diving' notices will be prominently displayed in all pools or areas of pools where there is a vertical depth of less than 1.5 m. Key safety points to remember are:

- check that the minimum water depth for head-first entries is 1.8 m;
- check the distance between the pool side and the surface of the water (maximum 0.38 m);
- check the distance from the starting point to the opposite wall (minimum forward clearance 7.6 m);
- check that the diving area is clearly marked across the pool (for example with rope dividers).

Diving code

Before learning how to dive, it is important to know and understand the *diving code*. The code requires that divers:

- check the entry area is clear before starting to dive;
- always dive and glide with arms extended;
- swim away from the starting position and avoid crossing the path of another diver after resurfacing;
- work in pairs and observe partners carefully;
- avoid pushing;
- do not wear goggles.

Learning how to dive

Early stages

In order to develop sufficient confidence to submerge, glide under the water and return to the surface, activities such as those listed below can be practised standing in shallow water. They are designed progressively to accustom the learner to being underwater and eventually upside-down before attempting a head-first entry from the pool side.

- Hold on to the scum-trough or pool side, placing the face in the water and blowing bubbles.
- Pick up objects from the bottom of the pool (for example coloured rings, balls).
- Push and glide to the bottom of the pool and return to the surface by raising the head and pointing the hands upwards.
- Attempt handstands in waist-deep water.
- Spring over or through apparatus (hoop or float) from a standing position in the water with the arms extended above the head. Spring into a handstand or take a shallower, oblique entry into a glide.

When the learners can perform the above activities confidently, they are ready to progress to head-first entries from the pool side. When learning how to dive, a minimum depth of 1.8 m is required. It is essential that those being taught are confident and able to swim in the depth of water being used.

Diving progressions

Sitting dive

From a sitting position on the pool side, feet together resting on the trough, bend the body forwards with the head held down between outstretched arms. By raising the hips and leaning further forwards, overbalance into a shallow dive (*see* fig. 13).

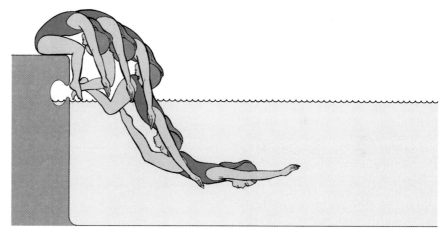

▲ *Fig. 13 Sitting dive*

29

Kneeling dive

In this dive, one foot is placed forwards, toes gripping the edge of the pool, and the other knee is placed alongside. Holding the head firmly between your upper arms, bend towards the water (still keeping the arms extended and the head down). From this position, raise the hips and allow the body to overbalance. Try to aim for the bottom of the pool. Stretch the legs on entering the water and glide back to the surface with arms extended (*see* fig. 14).

Crouch roll

This is the first of the standing dives. The diver stands quite close to the water, then crouches on the pool side with knees and feet together and toes gripping the edge. The hips should be high, and the arms pressed tightly to the ears pointing down towards the water. The chin rests on the chest. Maintaining this position, the body rolls forwards and reaches for the bottom of the pool. There is no push action – just a smooth roll (*see* fig. 15).

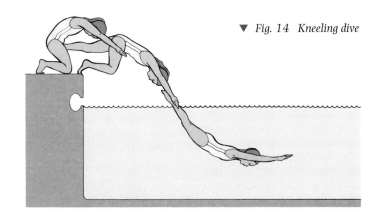

▼ *Fig. 14   Kneeling dive*

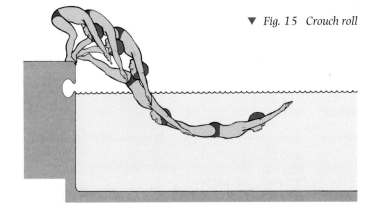

▼ *Fig. 15   Crouch roll*

Crouch dive

The diver's starting position is now more upright, knees bent together and toes gripping the edge of the pool. The upper arms are pressed firmly against the head, hands pointed downwards towards the water. The diver leans forwards so that the body overbalances; this is followed by a strong upward push from the feet through the hips. The diver should enter the water further away from the pool side than for the crouch roll, and the resulting glide is shallower (*see* fig. 16).

Lunge dive

The learner places one foot at the edge of the pool, toes gripping the edge. The other foot is stretched behind, toes just touching the floor. The body bends towards the water, keeping head and arms in line. By raising the rear leg and pushing from the front foot, the body overbalances. The rear leg controls the 'overbalance' and gives a good body-line. As the hands reach the water the front leg joins the other to give a good entry position. The aim should be to gain still more distance from the side.

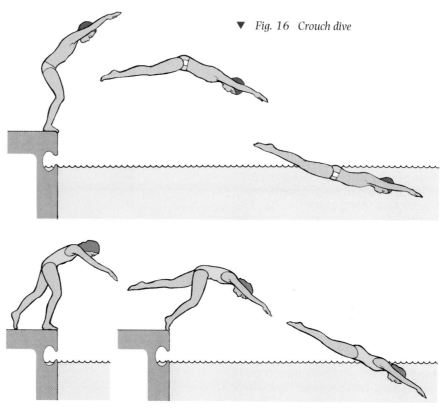

▼ *Fig. 16   Crouch dive*

▲ *Fig. 17   Lunge dive*

Plunge dive

Stand on the pool side, feet slightly apart and toes gripping the edge, with the body bent downwards but with the head raised so that the eyes look forwards and downwards towards the intended point of entry. Let the arms hang loosely down. When the body overbalances, swing the arms vigorously forwards, simultaneously thrusting the legs forwards strongly. During flight, the body should be fully extended and in a straight line in order to achieve a clean entry (*see* fig. 18). As this dive is commonly used for pool-side entries, it is worthwhile practising it until it can be performed competently.

Having achieved a good plunge dive the learner may wish to progress to board diving. By joining a diving club where there are good facilities and expert teaching it is possible to progress safely, and to enjoy the sport and the companionship. Membership of a diving club or the diving section of a swimming club can open up a whole range of competitive opportunities.

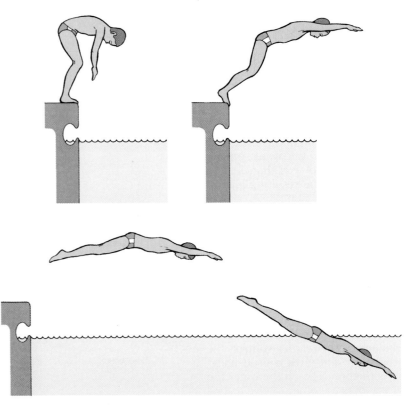

▲ *Fig. 18 Plunge dive*

Recreational swimming

In addition to the four main strokes already described, there are others that are no longer used in competition. They are well worth learning for recreational purposes or for their adaption and application to other activities in water (particularly lifesaving).

Elementary back stroke

Body position

Lying on the back, the swimmer takes up an almost horizontal position, face clear of the water. (If the head is raised a little, a lower leg position will result so that the knees are not likely to break the surface on recovery (*see* fig. 19a).

Leg action

The pathway of the leg action is similar to that of an inverted breast stroke, with the emphasis on flexed ankles so that the kick is felt to be made with the soles of the feet.

Bend the knees by dropping the lower legs (heels moving towards the seat). The heels should be hip-width or more apart, ready for the drive backwards. The thighs remain almost in line with the body just under the surface of the water. The position of the knees is relatively unimportant, although the distance between tends to be narrow rather than wide (*see* fig. 19b). On completion of the recovery, the feet are flexed and turned out ready for propulsion (*see* fig. 19c).

Propulsion

With the heels well apart and the ankles flexed, the drive is slightly outwards and backwards. The feet move through a circular pathway, and the inside borders as well as the sides of the feet push against the water to gain propulsion (*see* fig. 19e). In the final phase the legs come together to form a streamlined position for the glide (*see* fig. 19f). The legs may or may not move together depending on the activity for which the stroke is intended.

Arm action

This might be described as a wide sculling action.

The hands are kept under the water and move simultaneously, being pulled upwards, close to the body, from thigh to chest (*see* fig. 19b). They are then swept sideways until the arms are extended in line with the shoulders, in preparation for the propulsive action (*see* figs 19c and d).

Propulsion

With the palms of the hands gaining purchase on the water, the extended arms are pressed strongly backwards and inwards towards the sides of the body (*see* figs 19e and f).

Breathing

The face is clear of the water throughout the stroke. Normally, breath would be taken on recovery and exhaled with propulsion.

Timing

This is fairly simple. Leg movements tend to precede arm actions, but they appear to be simultaneous. There is no pause between the end of recovery and the beginning of propulsion. A glide may be performed with the body held in an extended position at the end of the propulsive actions.

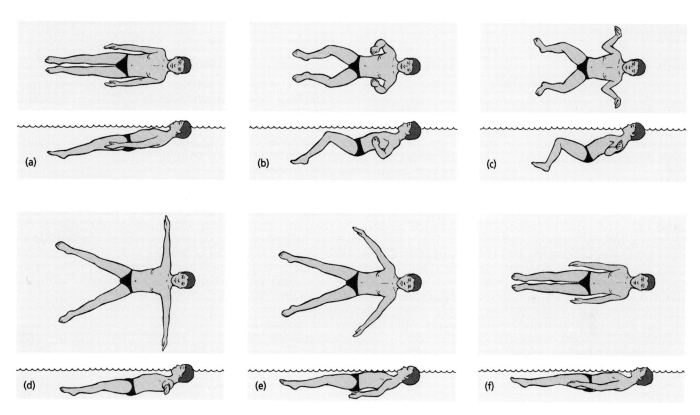

▲ *Fig. 19   Elementary back stroke viewed from the side and from above*

Side stroke

Body position

As the name suggests, the swimmer lies in the water, on either side, in as streamlined and horizontal a position as possible. The side of the head is in the water; the eyes and nose are just above the surface (*see* fig. 20a).

Leg action

The legs move simultaneously, one above the other and extended. The upper leg moves forwards and the lower leg moves backwards, with the knees bending and the heels moving towards the seat (*see* fig. 20b). Propulsion occurs as the legs are swept together through a circular pathway (*see* fig. 20c) back to the extended position which is held during a glide (*see* fig. 20d). The action is sometimes called a 'scissor' kick.

Arm action

During the glide the upper arm lies along the upper side of the body, and the lower arm is extended forwards in advance of the head (*see* fig. 20a). From these positions the arms move simultaneously. The upper arm recovers as it moves forwards to a position with elbow bent and hand below the head. At the same time the lower arm propels by pulling in a downward–sideways direction to meet the other arm, in a similar position, with elbow bent and the hand below the head (*see* fig. 20c). Still moving simultaneously, and without pausing, the arms are now extended with the upper arm propelling as it pushes downwards–backwards, while the lower arm recovers as it extends to the forwards position (*see* fig. 20d).

Breathing

Inhalation normally takes place during the propulsive action of the lower arm which tends to raise the upper body and head. As the glide begins, exhalation takes place through nose and mouth.

Timing

While the arms are moving inwards to their bent positions, the legs recover from extended bent positions ready for the propulsive kick. This is accompanied by the extension of the arms. Then follows a short glide before the actions are repeated.

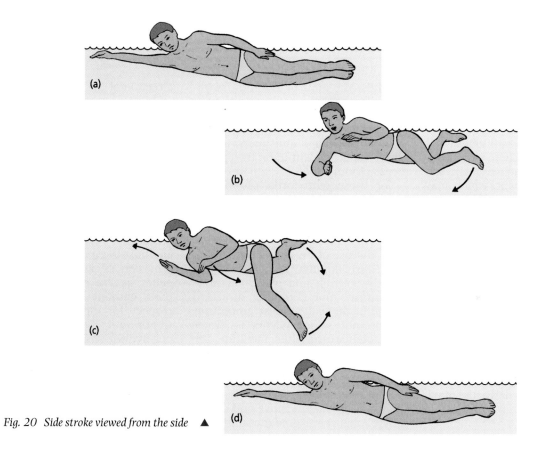

Fig. 20 Side stroke viewed from the side ▲

37

Swimming for people with disabilities

Water activities, and swimming in particular, are of considerable value to people with psychological, sociological and physical disabilities. Irrespective of the level or nature of the disability, it is possible for individuals to experience success, a sense of achievement and consequently enjoyment, which may not be possible in other situations or environments.

Many swimming pools have facilities and equipment that afford people with physical disabilities access to buildings, changing facilities and the pool itself. This enables them to experience a sense of worth and value.

It is important for those with disabilities to enquire (or to have someone ask on their behalf) about the provision of appropriately qualified teachers and assistants and the availability of water time. This makes it possible for them to derive the maximum benefit from any programmes of water activities.

Whilst the aims of teaching swimming are the same for all persons, with or without disability, teaching methodology and actual programme content will vary and, more importantly, be dependent upon the specific needs of individuals.

For those with forms of physical disability, whether or not these are accompanied by other difficulties, basic safety skills must be taught with care. These include: safe entry and exit with the use of an appropriate lifting procedure; flotation; recovery to a safe resting position and place; rhythmic breathing; and changing direction whilst in the water. These procedures will promote self-confidence and water competence and thus facilitate the learning of swimming skills.

The use of helpers and assistants, both in and out of the water, is invaluable in promoting skill-learning, since they can provide sensitive and appropriate support and guidance under the direction of the pool-side teacher.

Whilst specific disabilities will require individual approaches, there are a number of general activities which are useful. These include: bobbing and breathing; water adjustment and floating; perceptual motor activities; basic safety skills; swimming skills; and games activities with and without music.

Successful learning by people with disabilities will be enhanced by emphasising a number of factors: the provision of as many water experiences as are normally available to those without any form of disability; respect for each disabled person's worth and dignity; an empathetic, positive and smiling approach in order to reduce fear and anxiety levels; and, at all times, a concern for safety. Flexibility of approach is essential, as is the understanding that for many individuals a first visit to the swimming pool will be a traumatic time with anxiety manifesting itself in varied behaviours – excitement, aggression, tears, withdrawal.

Guided discovery and movement exploration are invaluable methods of teaching because they provide a sound foundation of general water skills and competence and thus facilitate the development of specific swimming skills.

Membership of a swimming club will further reinforce the concept of equality for individuals with disabilities and special needs, providing further opportunities for companionship and friendship, further development of swimming strokes and skills, and, for those who have the desire, competition. The ASA has a policy of equality for all.

Water safety

Water safety is the promotion of understanding how to be safe in and near water. It is one of the important aspects of swimming included in the National Curriculum, some aspects of which can be taught in the home or classroom away from the pool environment. Safety training can be started before the first visit to the pool if children are old enough to understand the principles. The subject may be approached in a manner which offers interest and challenge to children, allowing them to use their imagination regarding potentially dangerous situations. Links with environmental issues may also be raised through questions and activities on the subject of safety in and around local expanses of water such as ponds, quarries, docks, canals and clay-pits. The principles associated with water safety may be reinforced at any time the children are near an expanse of water or when a favourite television programme involves some aquatic activity.

As an example of how children may be encouraged to think about the dangers of water, teach the rules outlined on page 40 (and any additional ones considered appropriate) and then ask questions on specific situations to reinforce them.

Rule	Related questions	Rule	Related questions	Rule	Related questions
When playing in or near water always ensure that a competent older person is with you.	Why is it a good idea to swim with other people? Which places are safe for swimming? What is a safe number of people to go swimming?	Do not stand on the edge of a soft bank of a river, lake or stream.	What could happen if you stand on the edge of an over-hanging river bank?	Learn the safety rules for swimming pools.	Why is it dangerous to run along the side of a pool? What might happen if you push some-one into a pool? What should you do before diving into a pool?
If you are in trouble in water, relax, roll on to your back, and if you see somebody wave with one arm to attract attention. Otherwise, keep your arms under the water.	What is the least tiring way of keeping your head above water? If someone in the water is waving with one hand, what could it mean?	If you feel cold or tired in the water, get out immediately.	What could happen if you stay in very cold water? What could happen if you stay in water when you are tired?		
		Never dive into unknown water.	What is meant by unknown water? How should you enter unknown water?		
Learn the beach flag code.	What colour flags mark safe swim-ming areas? What colour flags suggest dangerous water?	Don't use air beds in open water.	What may happen to an air bed in open water? How can an air bed be used more safely?		
Don't go swimming in the hour after a heavy meal.	Why is it unwise to swim straight after a meal?	Always make sure the water is safe before entering it.	What steps would you take to ensure that a stretch of water is safe before you go into it?		

It may prove helpful to involve children in producing a list of rules which can be displayed as simple wall-charts for home or classroom use.

Photographs can be used to stimulate discussion about potentially hazardous bathing areas. For example, while studying a photograph of a very attractive and inviting area of open water, children might be asked to explain the checks they would make before getting in, how they would get in, and when they would come out of the water. Alternatively, they could suggest and act out dramatic situations involving some aspect of water safety.

Survival

Over half the people who drown in and around Great Britain every year are within about 25 m of land and therefore of reaching safety. If all those who take part in water-based activities were aware of the basic principles of survival, and could swim with confidence for about 50 m, the number of deaths from drowning could be drastically reduced. Most drownings do not occur as a result of swimming activities but arise as a result of what might be described as 'fooling about' near water. Another important factor to consider is that boys are far more likely to be involved in drowning accidents than girls. All of this explains why swimming and water safety are vitally important and why the writers of the National Curriculum have included swimming, water safety and survival in the Programmes of Study for Key Stage 2.

How long anyone can survive in cold water depends upon several factors:

- the physical and physiological characteristics of the individual;
- the temperature and speed of flow of the water;
- the distance from safety;
- the expertise of any assistance available;
- the swimming ability of the individual.

Research carried out by the Royal Navy and others indicates that even strong swimmers are only able to swim in cold water for short periods of time (and consequently over short distances) and that the colder the water the shorter the distance. Depending upon a victim's reaction to cold shock, the maximum distance for swimming in water with a temperature around 4 or 5°C is 150 m.

Cold shock

Cold shock (cardio-respiratory reflex response) is the name given to the effects that sudden immersion in cold water has on the body's systems. These effects are similar but more extreme than those experienced when standing under a very cold shower. Indeed, standing under a cold shower is one method used for training to withstand the effects of cold shock. Children may like to experience the effects of cold shock as part of their education, but they should not be compelled to take part nor be permitted to compete for the longest stay.

Sudden immersion in cold water causes a very rapid increase in the breathing rate (*hyperventilation*) which can be as much as five or six times faster than normal. At the same time, blood pressure increases; this is accompanied by a narrowing of the blood vessels near the surface of the skin (*vasoconstriction*). This, the body's normal reaction to a reduced surface temperature, causes a further increase in blood pressure. The combination of all these physiological effects is to increase the output of blood from the heart by as much as 30 per cent (or even more in some people). For many people, especially those who are less fit physically, this may be fatal. The physiological reaction of the body to very cold water is much more severe and death would occur in a much shorter period of time.

Action in an emergency

Sudden immersion in cold water requires the 'casualty' to react quickly and confidently. Parents and teachers have a very important responsibility in encouraging this degree of confidence.

The first action to be taken must be to reduce the effect of cold shock by getting the breathing rate to return to near normal as quickly as possible. This is achieved through deep, slow, controlled breathing while holding a floating object. Where no floating object is available the only alternative may be to tread water using a slow, steady movement similar to the breast stroke leg action but in an upright position.

The casualty must then assess the degree of danger from other sources such as oil, petrol or falling debris. Where such danger exists, the casualty should swim away calmly and confidently using a breast stroke action.

Having reached relative safety it should be possible to assess if any assistance is likely to be available close at hand, and then to attract attention by using the International Distress Signal. While treading water repeatedly raise one arm from an outstretched sideways position to a vertical position.

Where an emergency arises a few metres from the bank of a river or lake, the calm, confident swimmer should be able to take action to reduce the effects of cold shock and then wade or swim to the bank. However, it must be emphasised that, even in comparatively shallow water which is very cold, the effects of cold shock may be fatal for young children or older people.

Commonsense rules for open water

- Always use an approved life-jacket when taking part in water sports.
- If a boat upturns, stay with it until help arrives.
- In an emergency away from the bank, retain as much clothing as possible. Remove only waterlogged garments which may cause submersion.
- Keep the head above water as much as possible, and where possible use a floating object for support.

Basic survival skills

Treading water

This skill enables the casualty to stay in a vertically upright position with the head above water. The most effective technique in a survival situation is a slow, steady breast stroke leg action while sculling with outstretched arms (*see* fig. 21).

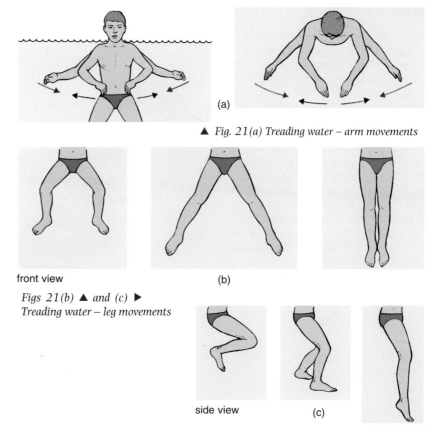

(a)

▲ *Fig. 21(a) Treading water – arm movements*

front view (b)

Figs 21(b) ▲ *and (c)* ▶
Treading water – leg movements

side view (c)

43

Stationary position

When a long distance from the shore, a casualty has a greater chance of survival by remaining motionless to conserve energy and waiting for help to arrive (*see* fig. 22). When a life-jacket is being worn, the legs should be kept together, the hands hooked into the collar of the life-jacket and the elbows close into the sides. The legs should be allowed to adopt a natural position, since it is found that with progressive shivering and the general increase in muscle tension the hips take up a natural position. In choppy water it may be necessary to alter the body position from time to time so that the back is against the oncoming waves.

Where no life-jacket is available, any floating object should be used so that a position approximate to that described above may be attained.

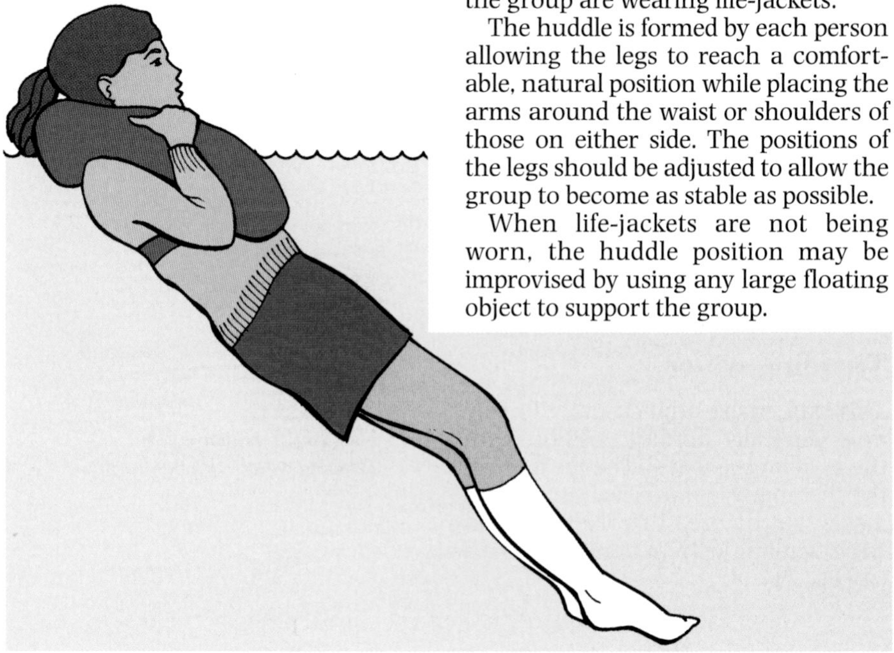

The huddle

A small group of people may collectively reduce heat loss by huddling together. This is more effective if all members of the group are wearing life-jackets.

The huddle is formed by each person allowing the legs to reach a comfortable, natural position while placing the arms around the waist or shoulders of those on either side. The positions of the legs should be adjusted to allow the group to become as stable as possible.

When life-jackets are not being worn, the huddle position may be improvised by using any large floating object to support the group.

▲ *Fig. 22 Stationary position*

Competitive swimming

Most people learn to swim as a means of keeping fit, as a pleasurable leisure-time activity, for safety reasons, or as a prerequisite for other water sports such as canoeing, sub-aqua, sailing or wind surfing. Some are endowed with a high degree of natural ability and aptitude; once they have achieved a degree of proficiency in one or two of the four main strokes, they like to compare their prowess with others and so become attracted to competitive swimming. However, this is not an easy option; great dedication, self-discipline and motivation are required in order to reach high levels of performance.

Requirements

- A practical knowledge of swimming skills, stroke techniques and methods of training.
- Physical fitness. As well as skill and the right mental attitude, a swimmer needs strength, suppleness, endurance.
- A determination and willingness to work hard; the discipline of training will give lasting benefits to swimmers who are fit to undertake it.
- A healthy lifestyle with regular habits of eating, working and sleeping.

Training methods

Successful swimming coaches employ a variety of methods in order to enable swimmers to realise their potential. Programmes will emphasise sound technical performance, the development of endurance through distance swimming, and strength and power (using speed work in the water as well as land conditioning). One of the principles of training is gradually to increase the workload as well as the number of repetitions of particular exercises.

A typical programme might take the following form.

- Warm-up swim to prepare muscles, heart and lungs for the more strenuous work to follow.
- Isolated practices (arms only; legs only) for strength and endurance and to concentrate on aspects of technique.
- Full-stroke swimming. As fitness improves, distances and times can be varied and increased, with intervals set as required.
- Starts and turns – these can be of considerable advantage if performed well in competition, since they may make the difference between winning or losing a race.
- Loosening-down swim to allow the body to return to normal functioning. (It is better to leave the water feeling pleasantly tired rather than completely exhausted.)

Land conditioning

Although most training for swimming is done in the water, many swimmers also use some form of land conditioning to develop the strength, power, endurance and mobility required to improve their level of fitness for competitive swimming. Such conditioning might include the following.

- Weight training – helps to develop strength, power and endurance.
- Pulley work – using special apparatus, the main muscle groups can be exercised.
- Circuit training – involves moving through a series of different exercises designed to increase strength and endurance.
- Mobility exercises – to increase the range of movements in the main joints.
- Energetic games – add variety in addition to developing general physical fitness (volleyball, squash, badminton, basketball).

Swimming clubs

Initially, a swimmer may wish to practise and train alone. However, as progress is made, the time will come when expert advice and guidance will be needed. This is the time to join a swimming club. Where there is a pool, there is usually a club; membership is comparatively inexpensive. Joining a club has many advantages:

- advice and guidance from qualified coaches and teachers;
- working to specifically prepared training programmes;
- working with others of equal ability;
- the use of apparatus and equipment;
- facilities for competition;
- making new friends and enjoying social occasions with club members.

Competitions

- Internal swimming-club events.
- Inter-club and league events.
- Age-group competitions at ASA area, county and district levels (these allow swimmers to compete against others of their own age group; events are arranged to cover all four strokes over distances from 50 m in the youngest group to 800 m and 1500 m in the oldest group; the advantage is that swimmers are not exposed at too early an age to competition against much older swimmers; by meeting qualifying times set annually by the ASA it is possible to compete in the National Age Group Championships).
- National competitions (in addition to the National Age Group Championships, there are two main National events: (i) the short course championships, taking place in 25-metre pools; and (ii) the long course championships, also referred to as the National Championships).
- English Schools National Championships, for school children only.
- Masters Competitions which are open to swimmers aged 25 years and over.

Awards

There is no doubt that awards for swimming and allied aquatic activities act as an incentive to improve for all ages and abilities. The ASA provides the most comprehensive series of awards of any sport in Britain and beyond. The awards recognise the need to reward achievement, from an infant's first movement through the water to competency at higher levels of aquatic skill. They cover all aspects of aquatic activity usually associated with swimming, including the basic skills required for diving, synchronized swimming, water polo, survival, distance awards for young improvers and middle-distance awards catering specifically for adults. For those people with permanent disabilities, the ASA permits variations in the regulations of most awards to enable them to be taken under conditions as near normal as possible. Throughout the complete range of awards, emphasis is placed on safety and skill.

Comprehensive and up-to-date information on the award schemes may be obtained from the ASA Director of Education, Amateur Swimming Association, Harold Fern House, Derby Square, Loughborough, Leicestershire, LE11 5AL (tel: 01509 618722).

Index